Real Estate

Reliable Strategies for Consistently Making Profit When Investing in Real Estate

By George Edwards

© **Copyright 2015 by George Edwards- All rights reserved.**

This document is geared towards providing exact and reliable information in regards to the topic and issue covered. The publication is sold with the idea that the publisher is not required to render accounting, officially permitted, or otherwise, qualified services. If advice is necessary, legal or professional, a practiced individual in the profession should be ordered.

- From a Declaration of Principles which was accepted and approved equally by a Committee of the American Bar Association and a Committee of Publishers and Associations.

In no way is it legal to reproduce, duplicate, or transmit any part of this document in either electronic means or in printed format. Recording of this publication is strictly prohibited and any storage of this document is not allowed unless with written permission from the publisher. All rights reserved.

The information provided herein is stated to be truthful and consistent, in that any liability, in terms of inattention or otherwise, by any usage or abuse of any policies, processes, or directions contained within is the solitary and utter responsibility of the recipient reader. Under no circumstances will any legal responsibility or blame be held against the publisher for any reparation, damages, or monetary loss due to the information herein, either directly or indirectly.

Respective authors own all copyrights not held by the publisher.

The information herein is offered for informational purposes solely, and is universal as so. The presentation of the information is without contract or any type of guarantee assurance.

The trademarks that are used are without any consent, and the publication of the trademark is without permission or backing by the trademark owner. All trademarks and brands within this book are for clarifying purposes only and are the owned by the owners themselves, not affiliated with this document.

Disclaimer – Please read!

The information provided in this book is designed to provide helpful information on the subjects discussed. This book is not meant to be used, nor should it be used, to diagnose or treat any medical condition. For diagnosis or treatment of any medical problem, consult your own physician. The publisher and author are not responsible for any specific health or allergy needs that may require medical supervision and are not liable for any damages or negative consequences from any treatment, action, application or preparation, to any person reading or following the information in this book. References are provided for informational purposes only and do not constitute endorsement of any websites or other sources. Readers should be aware that the websites listed in this book may change.

Buy land, they're not making it anymore.

-- Mark Twain

Table of Contents

Introduction 7
The Winding Road of Real Estate 9
   Booms and Busts 9
   Nothing Down 11
   Late Night Infomercials 12
   Your Own Pace 13
Are You a Good Fit for the Real Estate Investing Scene? 15
   Your Why – Your Motivation 17
   Will REI Fit for You? 19
Bird-dogging Your Way to Your First Check 20
   Types of Real Estate Investing 20
   Earn While You Learn 22
   Where are Investors Found? 23
   What to do When You Get the Nod 24
Quick Flips – Wholesaling Houses 27
If I Had a Hammer – Ready to Rehab? 35
Buy-and-Hold and Landlord 41
   Want to be a Landlord? 43
Getting Your REI Self-Education 47
Who Are Your Team Players? 53
   When to Build Your Team 54
Will You Be Found? 65
Specialized Niches 75
Scaling Up 81
Show Me the Money 85
Conclusion 91

Introduction

Something about the title of this book – *Real Estate: Reliable Strategies for Consistently Making Profit When Investing in Real Estate* – must have caught your attention for some reason. Perhaps it's because it speaks of *reliable strategies*. After all, you've probably heard that many people in the last *economy bust* lost a lot of money in real estate. Or perhaps it was because it inferred that profits can be *consistent*. That too would be enough to turn heads. Or perhaps it's just because of the words *real estate*. That subject, in and of itself, can be pretty intriguing.

Whatever the reason, I'm glad you decided to pick up this book and venture on this journey to learn more about the business of real estate investing. It is simultaneously a complicated, complex, and also a simple and straight-forward business in which to be engaged.

Many people enter into the world of real estate investing unprepared, uneducated, and too eager to make a boatload of money. Dozens of *so-called* REI gurus stand ready to take your hard-earned money; to regale you with exaggerated promises that *their system* is the one that will take you to the top. Some of these tricksters are better at writing books than at real estate investing. They are more than ready to help you part with your money by selling how-to courses. This is not to say all real estate investing courses (and websites, etc.) are scams. They definitely are not. But how will you know the difference?

This book is not designed to sell you anything. Rather it's to be a guidebook to help you navigate through the sometimes murky waters of this interesting business.

You will want to beware of anyone who tries to sell you a one-size-fits-all real estate investing program. Their claim will be that their system is the one and only, the best thing out there, that it uses the most technologically advanced software, and on and on. The ads they produce may show people with viable checks from deals they have closed – and always due to the greatness of this particular program being offered.

The fallibility of this approach is that no two real estate investors (or newbie investors) are the same; no two have the same goals; no two have the same temperament. Hence the one-size-fits-all theory goes out the window.

Another problem lies in the fact that many people who are now outside the business simply assume the way to get started in real estate investing is to buy property. Believe it or not, that is *not* the best way to get started. But more about that later in the book.

And yet another problem arises when the newbie is convinced that since he bought his house (perhaps has bought and sold two or three residences), he's convinced that this real estate business can't be all that difficult. So he jumps in with no training or education and subsequently gets slaughtered.

It doesn't have to be that way. There are wise and prudent ways to come into real estate investing; ways that are profitable and very nearly risk free.

Hopefully, I've given enough in this introduction to allow you to see that there's more to the real estate investing business than first meets the eye.

And hopefully, your curiosity has been piqued enough to compel you to keep on reading.

If so, let's get started.

*[**NOTE**: In spite of the fact that there are hundreds of successful women in the business of real estate investing, I have chosen to use all male gender references in this book. The sole reason for this is to avoid repeatedly using the he/she option, or switching back and forth from one to the other, which becomes awkward and confusing.]*

The Winding Road of Real Estate

Booms and Busts

Throughout the history of the U.S., we have seen periods of real estate speculation, and also periods of booms and busts in the real estate sector of the economy.

In the 1800s for example, land speculators rushed in to purchase parcels of land in a small frontier town on the basis of rumors that the railroad was headed their way. Who knew that a few decades later the presence of the railroad would make little or no difference in the value of the land?

Who knew that the onslaught of the Great Depression would drive foreclosures through the roof and many who owned properties (thinking they were in a safe position) lost everything?

Closer to home (time-wise), we need look no further than the most recent boom and bust of 2007-2008. Many investors at that time were buying up houses because 1) the terms were easy, and 2) the prices just kept going up. That is, until they stopped going up. What a reality check that was.

Ask anyone who invests in stocks – the timeworn saying is so true – *what goes up must come down.* And in this case it was true of real estate.

Through the mid-1990s and into the early 2000s, mortgages were made available to many who were of questionable financial stability. Hundreds and thousands of subprime loans were soon going into default.

Banks that had made the unwise decision to make subprime mortgages their major business focus began to see late payments and defaults; so much so that those banks collapsed.

Next in line were the insurance companies that had insured these mortgages. Then the financial institutions that were the underwriters for the loans were shut down and they brought down others in their wake.

Meanwhile, in neighborhoods across the country increased foreclosures brought down values of nearby homes, hence the fallout spread across the country from 2008 to around 2010.

My purpose here is not to go back and rehash all the bad times, but rather to keep it fresh in our minds that entering into real estate with the mindset that prices are always going to increase is sheer folly.

Are the chances great that the values will increase? Yes. But if that's the sole basis of your real estate investing business plan, you may be headed for disaster. You would have just as much chance of making money at a casino in Las Vegas.

Nothing Down

Robert Allen burst on the scene in the early 1980s with a book called *Nothing Down*. Basically, he just described 50 techniques for buying property with no money. Some would later say that Allen was better at selling (books) than at buying (real estate). Be that as it may, he started a phenomenal marketing bonanza. He held conventions in major cities where authors of various real estate investing techniques spoke to the large crowds. Their main focus was the book table (cassette-tape table) at the back of the room. Millions of dollars of teaching materials were sold during the three-day conventions. This ushered in what became known as, "The *Nothing Down* Real Estate Movement" of the 1980s.

Late Night Infomercials

Almost like a tag team came the emergence of late night *infomercials* from those who appeared to be *in the know* regarding real estate investing. Similar to Robert Allen, the idea was that the man-on-the-street could, with very little money, leverage their way into the exciting (or so they said) world of investing.

On the heels of the infomercials, they, too, would come into a city, set up an all-day seminar in a hotel meeting room, advertise widely, and draw a large crowd. (This was on a smaller scale than Allen's) Everyone, it seemed, wanted to get in on the act.

The prices of their *courses* were in the thousands of dollars. But if you were expecting to make multiple thousands in real estate it was considered a good investment.

It can be compared to the 1920s when it was touted that everyone from the mayor to the dogcatcher could buy stocks and make a killing. Like sheep to the slaughter, the *killing* came in a different form than expected.

Likewise when the bust of 2007-2008 hit, many green, uninitiated wanabe real estate investors sunk like a rock. They were overextended and unable to stay afloat during the crash.

Your Own Pace

This book will present a step-by-step journey into real estate investing that is safe and profitable. You can learn at your own pace, and avoid getting in over your head.

As the title for this chapter suggests, real estate investing can present to you a winding road. There can be obstacles, chug holes, detours, and dead ends. But if you are well prepared (mentally, emotionally, and financially), you can make it!

In the next chapter, you can take a look at whether or not you're a good candidate for setting up your own real estate investing business.

Are You a Good Fit for the Real Estate Investing Scene?

Some people have a plan to purchase a property in addition to their own residence and use it as a rental property. They may or may not, at a later time, add yet another. This individual is looking to make a little extra on the side in rent income. He has no desire to get into real estate investing as a full-time endeavor. You may know someone in this category.

This is not the person this book is set up to address. This book is written for the person who is perhaps miserable in the present work situation and wants a way out.

Or is looking for a lifestyle change

Or desires more time for family (or travel or whatever)

Or better education for the children

And the list goes on…

Does that describe you? No matter what the goal may be, it requires added income and you're thinking that perhaps real estate investing might just be the answer. But you're not totally sure.

As you move through this book, be assured that you will have a much clearer perspective. You will be able to make an informed decision based on your criteria, your goals, and your personality. (Quite the opposite from falling prey to one who is trying to sell you an expensive course, trying to convince you there's only one way to REI success. Which is *their way*.)

You Are Here

When you enter into a large mall, you'll see a big map of the entire place with an arrow indicating "you are here." Without that indicator, the map is useless. If you don't know in proximity to the mall, exactly where're you're located, you have no idea which way to turn to reach your intended destination. You may wind up in the Sears store when you wanted the bookstore. Your only solution would be to start out walking, meandering, looking, searching, but never really sure if you're getting closer or farther away from your destination.

It's the same way in life. You may have heard the adage:
If you don't know where you're going,
how will you know when you get there?

Let's apply this to your desire to enter into real estate investing and to make it a success. Where are you now? Where do you want to go? What will it take to get your there?

Then let's add one more very important question:
Why do you want to go there?

Your Why – Your Motivation

Later in the book I will be presenting some of the more common mistakes that newbie real estate investors tend to make. But for now at this juncture, motivation must be emphasized. Your ***why*** will be tested many times during the course of operating in the area of real estate investing.

For instance, the person who sees an ad that gives them the idea that they can make a quick buck (or a quick few-thousand bucks) trying their hand at REI will be one of the first ones to fold when the challenges rear their ugly heads. (And they will.)

This individual is simply *trying* to go this route; there is no deep heartfelt commitment. And their motivation to make a little extra money is too weak to carry on through a storm.

What is your *why*?

Block off a few hours where you can be alone – no distractions – with a notebook and pencil (or your laptop if you like to make notes electronically). If you've never created your life's plan, now is an excellent time to do so.

Begin making notes. Notes about:
- What you most enjoy doing
- What your perfect day would look like
- Where you want to be in a year – five years – ten years
- Describe your main life goal
- List your most prevalent weaknesses (actually, they may not be weaknesses at all, but just not in your personality type)
- List your most prevalent strengths (if you can't be objective here, ask a few trusted friends)

This may take a few separate alone-times. The more you compile this list, the more things will come to your mind. Sometimes we get so busy with life, we forget to ask ourselves what we would *really* like to do with our lives. Give yourself permission to dream.

The more vivid your goals, dreams, and visions, the stronger will be your inner motivation to take action when and where action is required. (This is your strong motivational **why**.)

Once you have this foundational information clarified in your mind (and heart), now it's time to bring real estate investing into the scenario.

Will REI Fit for You?

As you look over your list can you envision REI fitting in your life? Can you see yourself committing to whatever it takes to build your own REI business? Does your personality line up with what this kind of life requires? (More about exactly what is required later on in our journey through this book.)

For instance,
- Are you a self starter? (Or do you need a boss telling you what to do each day?)
- Are you a good money manager?
- How about people skills? Can you quickly make someone feel comfortable on the phone or in their presence?
- Where do you rank in communication skills? A great deal of interaction is required in this business from buyers and sellers, to realtors, to attorneys, to bankers, to contractors, and so on.
- Do you have a thirst for learning? Are you eager to learn new ways of doing things?
- How's your computer knowledge? You will at least need to know how to set up a website and send emails. (More about this in a future chapter.)

These are just a few things you might want to consider as you move forward. Let me quickly add that many traits and personality qualities can be developed. For instance, you may not be all that proficient in math skills; however, there are simplified formulas, there are calculators, and there are mentors and guides to walk you through the math side of things.

You can gain computer skills. You can train to improve communication skills. Again, when your motivation is strong, much of the nitty-gritty can be worked through. The important thing is for you to know when you need assistance and not to be too prideful to seek help.

In Chapter 3, you will be introduced to a unique way to get your feet wet in the world of real estate investing.

Bird-dogging Your Way to Your First Check

Want to be a bird dog? Sounds kind of silly when taken literally. But I'm being totally serious. This is a marvelous way to get started in this business. But before I divulge all the details of this endeavor I want to digress momentarily.

Types of Real Estate Investing

The phrase *real estate investing* is thrown around loosely, and yet it can take in a multiplicity of opportunities under this one umbrella. This is why people can get so confused when they read the glitzy ads that promise the moon.

One ad might show a multi-million dollar mansion from which they pocketed millions. You don't know until you read the fine print that this is a course teaching about short sales. Let me tell you, there's nothing quick or easy about working in short sales. Or it might be a course teaching specifically about probate deals. But this is yet another more specialized field in real estate investing. Here is a list of several types of investment methods:

- Wholesaling
- Fix and flip
- Fix and hold
- Buy and hold (rent)
- Probate properties
- Foreclosures
- Pre-foreclosures
- Short sales

This is not an extensive list, but it gives you an idea of what a smorgasbord is available. Is it no wonder that folks get confused?

Two Ways to Get Started

There are two basic ways to get started in real estate investing. One is to spend money; the other is to earn money. My suggestion is to take the route of the latter.

Now if you have tons of money and aren't sure where to spend it, be my guest. You can go with the first. But having a large sum of money to plunk down on a property, and having the wisdom and expertise to know if it's even a winning deal, is like night and day. Complete opposites. If you don't know the difference you can lose money at lightning speed.

Earn While You Learn

Now that you know what's going on in this world of REI, let's return to the subject of becoming a bird dog.

The common definition of a bird dog is a hunting dog that goes out ahead of the hunter and sniffs out the game. These dogs will flush out the game whereas if he were on his own, the hunter might never know they were there.

A real estate investor leads a busy life with many tasks to complete. The bigger his business grows, the less time he has to go out finding properties in which to invest. He needs someone to go and sniff out potential deals for him. He is more than willing to pay a few hundred dollars for this service (for a bird dog service), because it could net him a much bigger profit. This is called a *finder's fee* and it's usually about $500. Sometimes more, depending on the investor and the deal.

This is a perfect way for you to step into the world of REI. There's no risk, no big investment (all you need is a vehicle, gas, and time), no negotiating with a seller. You look for properties, take photos, make notes and email the information back to the investor for whom you are working. If the investor closes that deal, you get paid.

While you're earning cash, you are also learning more about real estate investing.

Where are Investors Found?

Now that you understand what a bird dog is and what it entails, the next step is to find investors who need your services.

As you are driving around through your community, keep an eye out for signs that say something like: "I buy houses." Usually there will be a phone number and a URL for a website. Connect with this person to see if they are now in the market for a bird dog.

Next, you can check out the local listings on CraigsList and look for ads that appear to be listed by an investor. They might look like this:

- "We buy houses all cash"
- "We buy houses and close fast"
- "We buy all houses as is – cash"
- "Sell Your Home NOW!"
- "We buy houses – fast cash and quick closing"

You can do the same with classified ads. You can also run a Google search for your city, and the same keywords as suggested above.

Create your list and make a few phone calls. Keep good notes. If they're not ready to take you on right now, they may be in the future. Follow up in a few weeks.

Yet another way to locate active investors in your areas is to attend meetings where they hang out. Ever hear of REI groups or clubs? Below are the sites of two such organizations. You can do a search on their sites to see if there is a group meeting near you. Find out where they meet and when – then make it a point to attend. Here you will meet the investors who need the services of a bird dog. Mingle and network. Ask lots of questions. Gather business cards and follow up.

- http://www.nationalreia.com/
- http://www.reiclub.com/

What to do When You Get the Nod

When an investor gives you the nod and turns you loose to begin bird-dogging for him, you'll want to find out exactly what he's looking for. What are his favorite zip codes in which to buy? What size houses? What price range? Exactly what information does he want?

If you are serious about this endeavor; if you are willing to go the extra mile for this investor; if you display integrity and dependability; you will make yourself indispensible. Who knows where such a road might lead.

When you're with this investor ask as many questions as you possibly can. Perhaps you can ride along when he looks at the property; or when he negotiates the deal with the seller. If opportunities arise where you can be a type of apprentice, grab that opportunity.

Keep in mind your job is to sniff out properties that are under the radar. You aren't scraping them off the MLS. You are driving the neighborhoods. You're asking the neighbors who live there; you're learning about the character of the neighborhood.

At first it may seem like searching for the proverbial needle in the haystack. But realize that the more you do this, the more you know what you're looking for and the more adept you'll be at finding exactly what your investor is looking for.

Get Serious

A word of warning. Just because this sounds super simple, don't view it as a sort of slap-dash, stop-off on your way to stardom. Take your job seriously. You are bringing a great deal of value to the table. You are increasing your investor's chances of growing his business.

You can have business cards made; you can put your own ads on CraigsList. Let people know what you're doing so that word spreads. Treat this like a business.

As an interesting side note, there have been those who made a full-time career in this phase of REI. They enjoyed the steady income, the flexible hours, and yet, the freedom from extensive paperwork and legal concerns.

In other words, the role of being an excellent bird dog perfectly fit their goals and their personality.

Now you understand why I said you can come into the world of REI making money or spending money. Being a bird dog is one of the best ways to step into the arena, to learn and to earn.

In the next chapter, we'll take a look at the next step up in relatively easy ways to earn without a great deal of risk – that is wholesaling. Check it out.

Quick Flips – Wholesaling Houses

Now that you have a clear picture of how to get started in REI by making money without going into debt – and by actually making money – we're turning our attention to the wholesaling arena.

What happens most often is that a person involved in bird dogging, once they get good at it and are able to do well at finding and recognizing houses that might be owned by a motivated seller, they realize they're ready to move up a notch. They've been working for wholesalers and they've witnessed how the wholesaling business actually works. Here's how that plays out.

The Typical Wholesaler

The typical wholesaler flips properties; they make money on houses they never own. Some transactions can actually close within a week; others may take a month or so. But it all happens very quickly. As with bird dogging, this is an excellent way to build up cash reserves without going into debt, and without making any long-term commitments.

The first step in wholesaling is to locate a distressed seller. This will be someone who desperately needs to sell the property that they own. There are a number of reasons that a person can be in this situation.

- A job transfer that has taken them away from the area (they may even be making two house payments).
- A divorce usually leaves homeowners in a precarious predicament
- Someone inherits a property – they don't want it and may even live out of state
- A family facing foreclosure and desperately needs to get out from under the pressure, and still save their credit
- The homeowner who simply over-bought and is overextended – they just want out

The list is pretty much endless, but you get the picture. The key ingredient necessary for a profitable flip is a sufficient amount of equity in the property.

Time to Negotiate

This homeowner may have contacted you in response to one of your ads. (More about marketing later in the book.) Or perhaps your bird dog scout brought the lead to you. Your next step is to set up a time to visit with the homeowner(s). This is when people skills and negotiating skills come into play. Another important aspect when getting the contract is your mindset. You must keep foremost in your mind that you are offering a viable, and much needed, service to this family. You are not out to harm them or to cheat them in any way.

You have already studied the ARV (after repair value) of the house, and you know what other houses in the areas are being sold for (the comps). This means you're in a position to wisely make your offer. You reiterate that you pay all cash and close quickly.

Let's say the offer is accepted (although sometimes the seller may have to think about it), you get a simple two-page contract signed right there on the spot. This is referred to as having it "under contract."

Word the contract so that you have 30 to 60 days to close – to give yourself breathing room. Following your name on the contract it will state *and/or assigns*. This means you have the right to *assign* this contract to another party. Pay a small deposit (it can be as little as $10.00) to secure the property.

The Title Company

You will already have a relationship built with a particular title company. This is your next stop. You must have the title checked to ensure there are no other liens against the property, or outstanding back taxes.

The Buyer

If the title is clean, you must have a buyer to take this property off your hands. Where are the buyers?

As you are building your wholesaling business, you will be on a constant lookout for buyers for the properties you put under contract. These buyers are investors who might be rehabbers. They love nothing more than getting their hands on a fixer-upper and making it look spiffy and new again.

The buyer might be someone who is deep into being a landlord. They have a string of houses that they rent out.

Or that buyer might be one who does lease options for interested buyers.

By attending REIA meetings, by hanging out with other investors, by using your website and venues such as social media you begin to build up a buyers list.

You can place ads in the *houses for sale* section of your local newspaper. Or you can use the local page of CraigsList. If you use key words such as "handy," "investor special," "needs work," and "distressed," you'll soon be fielding a lot of calls. Make sure you take the time to get their name and phone number and add them to your buyer's list. While you have them on the phone you can say something like:

I have properties like this quite often. Can you tell me what you're looking for? And in what area?

Add this information to your notes. They will be top of your list to call when the next house comes available.

As a wholesaler, you will always be adding to your buyer's list. In time, you will have such a great list (those buyers who know you and trust you), all you have to do is send out an email to your list describing the property you have under contract and almost immediately you will have those who are ready to step up and buy the property. This is how a wholesaler builds a strong business.

Getting Paid

Let's say your seller agreed to sell for $40,000. You are now in a position to assign this contract to the willing buyer. (You are in the middle.) You will now determine what you assignment fee will be for this service of bringing this contract to the buyer. The fees usually run about $5,000.

Keep in mind this buyer did none of the work to locate this property. You did all the work and now you are being paid for that work. You state that your fee is $5,000. This means you will be assigning the contract to the buyer for $45,000.

When the buyer agrees to this price and the assignment fee, you present the one-page form – the *assignment of contract*. (It is also called an *assignment of beneficial interest form*.) The contract states that you agree to give up any and all rights to purchase this property and that you are assigning it to the new buyer.

What Comes Next?

As you can see from the above, you are not really flipping properties at all – you are flipping contracts. You need not come up with any cash, and you pay no closing costs. When it's time to close you need not even be in the room. The closing company cuts you a check for the assignment fee, or wires you the money. The payment method will be established before the closing date.

Other than your time, attention, and energy, your only investment will be the $10 earnest money that you handed over to the seller to secure the deal.

Can you see why many investors settle into this niche and stay there? There are wholesalers who have converted this into a massive operation. They work virtually all around the country; they create large ad campaigns and put out mailings in the thousands. Often these are just simple postcards.

This may or may not be your niche, but you can see this is such a great way to accumulate cash reserves which will in turn enable you to move into a more complex niche.

The next chapter pulls back the curtain on the investor who chooses to rehab. Is this niche where you fit?

If I Had a Hammer – Ready to Rehab?

The Smell of Money

There are investors who can step into a run-down house that needs a ton of work and they smell *money*. While some see the mess, this individual can envision the finished product. As he walks through the house, he is already calculating exactly how much it will cost to get it into a salable condition. He can size up what needs to be done and how quickly it can be accomplished.

Most rehabbers hire outside contractors to do the grunt work. Although some may begin by trying to do it alone as a sort of do-it-yourself project, that usually will not last past the first property. (To their credit a beginning rehabber is usually cash-strapped. They see how much more profit can be made with a DIY approach.)

Too many pitfalls lie in wait once the work begins. That wallpaper that needs to be removed is pulling off the sheetrock. Leaky pipes in the basement spell more attention. The flue in the fireplace is faulty. And so on. Very quickly the rehabber will see that it's better to leave the hammering and painting to the experts.

Level of Rehab Needed

Each property will spell out a different level of needs in the way of fixing up. Some will have to be completely gutted. Others will need only cosmetic work – paint, new carpets, light fixtures, deep clean, and so on. As the rehabber, you will know which ones need what. Before you ever agree to make the purchase, you will have calculated the cash needed for the project. If it's too much, you simply back away from the deal and wait for better to come along.

Working with Contractors

When investors gather, one of their favorite pastimes is to compare contractor horror stories. They do abound. Contractors can be late, sloppy, irresponsible, and undependable. But they are absolutely necessary if you are going to rehab houses on a regular basis.

The biggest problem here is the time factor. You've heard the saying *time is money*. Never is it more true than in this scenario. The longer this house is in your hands, and is being repaired, and is not sold, it costs you in maintenance and upkeep. Utilities must be kept on throughout the work process.

If you are new in the business, you might be tempted to bring in the father-in-law of your first cousin on your mother's side to do the fix-up work. You've heard he's a pretty good handyman. Let me be brief here – **don't**. If it looks like a shortcut, it probably is not. You are headed for deep trouble – more trouble than you ever bargained for. Why take unnecessary risks?

Screening for the Best

First and foremost, your general contractor (GC) must be licensed, bonded, and insured. Do not take their word for it. Request to see proof. Check with the registrar of contractors to see if anyone has filed a complaint against this GC.

Ask for references and follow through to contact those references. Never go with the first bid. Always interview several.

This must be a company that is financially solvent. It's never a healthy thing to work with someone who is desperate to earn your business.

Set everything up on a pay-as-needed basis. Never (as in *NEVER*) pay the full price up front. You keep control of the cash and let that be the leverage you use. Make sure all the work passes your inspection before payout.

Many rehabbers go along with the contractor to purchase the supplies. This step could be eliminated later once a trust level has been established.

Determine who will pull the building permits; will the GC take care of that detail? Or will that be your job? Make sure that is clear and is stated in the contract.

Have your attorney draw up a binding contract and never start a project without the signed contract in your hands. If you ever have to go to court, you'll be thankful that you took this extra step.

Your Role

Once the work is underway, your role will be as the overseer. Never assume everything is going as it should. Guarantee it by making surprise visits to the project as it progresses.

As you get further into developing your investing business as a rehabber, you could have two or three projects going at once. All will require your continual oversight.

Time to Sell

You will need to be marketing to sell this property from the first moment you sign to make the purchase. Your goal is to turn it around as quickly as possible.

You may be selling to an investor looking for rental property. Or it may be the retail buyer – a family with a conventional loan ready to make a purchase.

Your website will be your showcase for the homes you have for sale. Before and after photos are always winners. You can also use social media, CraigsList ads, and the like. (More about marketing later in the book.)

Potential Income

I'm sure you've watched enough episodes of *Flip This House* to have heard some figures on the amount of money that can be made on a *fix-and-flip*. It can run anywhere from the tens of thousands to the hundreds of thousands. This is an extremely lucrative niche in real estate investing. It requires a greater level of expertise than simply wholesaling. Unlike being a wholesaler, you will be making rather large cash investments into the deal. You will need greater cash reserves, or you will need investors.

Now that you're more familiar with this niche you may feel that this is the exact fit for you.

In Chapter 6, we'll discuss yet a different approach, and that is the buy-and-hold niche for creating long-term wealth.

Buy-and-Hold and Landlord

When that rehabber gets that house all fixed up and ready to sell, it may go to the investor who is eager to build a little (or huge) empire of rental properties. Sometimes a rehabber will move over into rental properties simply because he has access to so many good deals. Instead of selling, he may hold two or three properties because he is savvy to the potential for cash flow.

As I mentioned earlier in the book, the main goal of buy-and-hold should not be hoping the property will increase in value. If it does, that is an added bonus. The best strategy for a rental is to establish a cash flow – more money should come in via the rent payments than the money that goes out for the mortgage payments (plus taxes and insurance). A percentage of the cash flow can be invested back into the business for upkeep and repairs.

Over time the rent pays down the mortgage and the equity just keeps increasing. Eventually some rental property owners will begin to use the equity in one house to purchase another – that's how the empire grows.

How to Finance

Early on, you probably will not have the wherewithal to purchase a property without financing. If you choose to go the route of traditional financing, you'll want to make sure you have a favorable credit rating. If this is a problem there are a number of reliable credit repair services available. Run a Google search for "credit repair service" and you'll find exactly what you need to get this little obstacle out of the way.

Want to be a Landlord?

The downside of this investing niche – or what most people perceive as the downside – is the role of being a landlord. Jokes abound about landlords being called out of bed at 2AM to go to the property and fix a plugged-up toilet.

Those who chose this niche have already reconciled themselves to this fact and are ready to take on the challenge. Overlooking the short-term inconvenience they have their eyes on the long-term rewards.

It's also true that some renters can literally trash a house. Again, the landlord who is game for this knows you simply call in the contractors and get it cleaned up, fixed up, and get it rented out again as quickly as possible. Minimize the down time and maximize the cash-flow time.

Maintain Your Cash Safety Net

If you are in the rental niche of investing, you must be wise about money managements. When a tenant leaves and the house is empty, the mortgage still needs to be paid. How long it will take for you to get the house refurbished and find a new tenant is an unknown. It's an unknown that you must be prepared to handle.

Property Management Company

For those who have too many houses to look after on their own will eventually hire a property management company to take care of those details. The management company will collect the rent, see to the upkeep, and will be the ones to answer the calls at two in the morning. And because most are reputable leasing agents, they will help you find new renters when the occasion calls for it. The better companies also are in touch with the best plumbers, electricians, and AC&H people in the area. This will take the worry off of you in this department. The management company will be the one fielding the calls for maintenance needs.

A word of caution here. A bad management company is worse than not having one at all. Hiring the wrong company could cost more than you're willing – or able – to pay. Be sure to get references and ask lots of questions. You might even want to have your attorney look over their contract to be sure you're protected.

Owning properties for rental purposes is the first thing pops into most people's minds when real estate investing is mentioned. This is because it's the most common; and for the uninitiated, it's pretty much all there is. Most people are not in the *inner sanctum* of the REI business and therefore are unaware of what all is available.

This is also how newbie investors get in into trouble. They overextend and for instance, if two or three houses should go empty all at once, they are at risk of going under. They'll be desperate to unload properties and will probably lose money in the process.

It doesn't have to be that way. This is why this book presents a different approach. Come into the business by making money and not going into debt.

In the next chapter, we'll go off the point a bit. We've covered some of the basic approaches to REI, but we haven't talked about how to educate yourself in the subject. Here are a few pointers.

Getting Your REI Self-Education

Locating the *Real Deal*

In the introduction, I mentioned that many so-called REI gurus are better at writing books (and creating courses) than they are at being successful real estate investors. This is not to say there are no reliable teachers (instructors, mentors) in the business, because there are. It's up to you to separate the wheat from the chaff. It's not that difficult to research to learn which ones are the *real deal*.

It's not the purpose of this book to name names or even to disparage anyone. The point is you *will* need to study and learn. It will be incumbent on you to self-educate. Yes, you can go out there on your own and you might make it. And you might fall flat on your face. Others have gone before you and walked through this journey; how much better it is to learn from their mistakes than making your own.

Begin with a Reliable Source

You may want to visit the site I mentioned earlier – http://www.reiclub.com/. An organization such as the REI Club can be trusted. On this site you will find a whole slew of resources. There are articles written by reputable and reliable investors. Some will offer their courses on the site, but the main purpose of the site is not for selling materials.

Visit Your Public Library

Make a list of some of these names you found at the REI Club site and then check your local public library. You may find books written by these investors. Here you can begin learning with no big cash outlay. After reading a few books, you'll know which investor you relate to and that will be the one you might want to choose to follow further.

Later, if (and when) you have the wherewithal, you can invest in a course that teaches about the niche in which you are most interested. Again, I stress that you go slow and not spend thousands on teaching materials. Believe me, there some of the *big names* out there that do charge thousands for their courses. And the way they tell it, theirs is the secret way (the surefire way; the only way) to make millions in real estate investing. My advice? Beware of hype!

Meet Investors Face-to-Face

You'll remember I suggested you find a REIA group in your area and begin attending the meetings. Many of these clubs will have a special speaker for each meeting. This is yet another great way in which to learn the ins and outs of the business. These will be investors who are out there in the trenches and have the war wounds to prove it. In this type of venue, you not only hear firsthand about experiences, you will also have the opportunity to ask questions afterward and perhaps even get to know that speaker. If it's a niche in which you are interested, you might offer to buy that speaker's lunch at a future date, and thereby learn even more.

Life-Long Learning

In this business, your education will never cease. You continue to learn every day that you are actively investing. Plus new laws and legislation can come along that will change the scene altogether. You must stay abreast of these.

In your goals notebook that you started keeping after reading Chapter 1 (you did start your notebook, right?), be sure to allot special blocks of time for your education. Even if you only spent one hour a week in learning (hopefully it will be more), you will have 52 hours of study to your credit by the end of one year. That's a lot of learning in anyone's estimation.

As you launch out into the REI world you will definitely be an entrepreneur; however, you cannot do this alone. You will need a whole team of players surrounding you. I'll introduce those players to you in the next chapter.

Who Are Your Team Players?

The so-called entrepreneurial spirit is awesome. It can propel a person out of their comfort zone and into new vistas and new adventures. However, there can also be a downside. Sometimes entrepreneurs are so driven and so compelled to *git-r-done*, as they say, they drive themselves into a state of exhaustion and burnout. It almost becomes a matter of pride that they can do all of this, can make it all work, and can totally be the star of their own show.

Such an attitude may be okay to an extent. It will certainly move you out of the herd mentality. At the same time, it's good to begin to develop a *CEO mentality*. You now have your own business and you are head of this business. One of the smartest things you can ever do is to realize where your expertise ends and the expertise of another begins.

In some cases, it might be a given. For instance most investors are smart enough to know they will need an accountant. The matter of filing a correct tax report is crucial to the health of your business. Other areas might not be so obvious.

Show me a successful real estate investor, and I'll show you a person who surrounds himself with a solid team of knowledgeable people – those with whom he works well, and whom he respects. In this chapter we're going to go over the possible players that you will want on your team.

When to Build Your Team

The time to begin building your team is before you ever need them. You will want to have these players in place as you are building your business. Why? Because it will take time to interview several candidates, to get to know them, and to find out if they are a right fit for your needs and your personality.

Once you have this list well in mind, you can be on the lookout for these individuals. You can ask for references and spend time selecting your key players.

Real Estate Agent

A lot of pros and cons go around about whether an investor will or will not need the services of a real estate agent. This is not a question that is answered with a yes or a no. Rather it's an "it all depends" answer.

First you must realize that just because a person holds a license does not mean they are proficient in the world of real estate. Learning the RE business takes many years of hard work and willingness to learn and grow. Such Realtors are few and far between.

To narrow the search even further, you want an agent who knows and understands all about how real estate investing works. Not only will they know how it works, they will *have an appreciation* for how it works. (Some Realtors view investors with a bit of disdain – sad, but true.)

Finding an agent who will work in tandem with you will gain advantages for both parties. It will truly become a win-win situation. Such agents are sometimes referred to as being *investor-friendly.*

Just because they may be few in number doesn't mean they're not out there. It just means you'll have to extend extra effort to make the connection. It may take a while, and it may require a bit of trial and error.

Situations could come your way that are not a right fit for you – they really need a Realtor. These can serve as leads for your agent-partner. Likewise, they will come across deals that could be a perfect fit for your investing business. Especially since that agent knows how your business operates. It becomes a reciprocal give-and-take.

This agent can get MLS information to you that you would not otherwise have access to, such as comps for a certain neighborhood.

They can also keep you updated on expired listings. Homeowners who have had their property listed for a time with no luck in selling might be eager to talk to an investor.

The Closing Agent

Those who are new to investing may see the closing agent as a minor role. They may think that all closing agents are alike. Mistake!

First of all let's look at what tasks a closing agent is responsible for. This person coordinates several activities that have to do with the completion of the sale of a property. The closing agent must ensure that all documents are properly filled out. Additionally, this individual sees to it that all funds are disbursed correctly. Because the agent acts as a custodian, it is a role that must be performed by a neutral party.

Ask to see if this agent will give you an investor discount on the escrow fees. This discount could be as much as 20%. Check for sure.

Your closing agent will be a very important member of your team, and you want one who will work closely with you. You want an agent who will give you their personal phone number in case you need to get hold of them over a weekend or after hours. As long as you do not abuse this privilege, your closing agent should be happy to do this.

Another wonderful feature about closing agents is that they know a lot of people in the world of real estate. What a great person to network with.

Once you get rolling in your investing business, you will be bringing a great deal of business to this agent – this means they should be more than happy to go the extra mile to work with you. But if not – then keep on looking. Don't minimize this member of your team.

General Contractor

We covered a number of details about hiring a general contractor in the chapter on rehabbing. To reiterate here, the main goal is to find a contractor who is licensed, bonded, and insured, and has the documents to prove it.

Let it be perfectly clear to the contractor that you do not pay up front – ever. Your arrangement will be to set up a disbursement plan, paying only as the work is completed and meets your standards.

Once you find a good GC, take good care of that person. Pay on time, keep your word, and give him a lot of business. If you are in the fix-and-flip niche, this team member has the power to make you or break you. You want it to be the former!

Inspector / Appraiser

Some people, especially if they are new in the business, may confuse the roles of the inspector and the appraiser. While they seem to be similar, they are different.

The inspector will cover the entire house – attic, basement, crawlspace, foundations, and every room – looking to find potential hidden problems. Some investors dread this part of the process; however, the smart investor will be a good student and learn from the inspector.

Once the inspection is completed ask to see a copy of his final report. Keep this in your files for future reference.

The inspector is a good person to get to know because they've been around a while and have experienced a wide variety of property problems. Make friends with the inspector because the two of you may work together quite often.

Check to see if your prospective inspector is certified. Several programs exist that offer certification. It's best to have an inspector who is credentialed.

While the inspector has to do with the physical construction and condition of the home, the appraiser is more concerned with the *value*. It will be the job of the appraiser to compare the seller's asking price to the price of similar homes that have recently sold in the neighborhood. These comparable prices (or comps) will help you in your negotiation process. You will want an appraiser who is experienced and comes with good references.

Real Estate Attorney

Your real estate attorney will be a crucial member of your team, because it only takes one frivolous lawsuit to wipe you out of business. It's no secret that we live in a litigious society where lawsuits abound. Add to that the fact that different states have different real estate laws which means all of your documents must be state-specific.

Early on in your business you will want to build a strong relationship with your RE attorney. As your business grows, you will want this person to review all of your documents – and do it for an affordable price.

And it's for this reason that your attorney must be familiar with all of the ins and outs of real estate investing. For instance you may need one who understands probate laws, or foreclosure laws, and so on. Preferably your attorney should be one who already has other RE investors as clients.

It's a good idea to interview several attorneys before you make your choice. It must be a good fit business-wise and on a personal level. You will need to *like* this person as you will be doing a lot of work together.

Accountant

If you want a quick recipe for disaster in your business, it would be lax bookkeeping habits. You are running a business and it cannot operate effectively and efficiently if you aren't sure how much is coming in and how much is going out.

Most of the investors that I come in contact with, highly dislike the task of *keeping the books*. It's for this reason that you must be shopping for an accountant before you need one.

A word of caution, avoid bringing an accountant on board just because an acquaintance recommended that person. Just as with your Realtor, and your attorney, you want someone who is familiar with the REI business.

This person will be responsible for your taxes, and possibly your tax planning strategies. This alone could save you a lot of money.

You will need to decide if you want weekly, monthly, or quarterly services – or only services at tax time. You also must know up front exactly how this accountant charges. Then there are no surprises.

After a few years in the business, you will be doubly thankful that you have a trusted accountant that you can rely on. It could mean the difference in whether or not your business remains solvent.

Insurance Agent

Next on our list of team players is your insurance agent. Here again, this person must (*must*) be a person who understands your business so your needs will be covered properly.

Something you will want to know early on is if this agent can offer same-day service. Once a property comes into your possession it will need to be insured. Your agent will need to cover both vacant and rental properties.

For the wholesaler, you need affordable temporary coverage to protect you in case of property damage or a lawsuit that might arise during construction.

As you search for this team player, make sure it is an independent agent. This is so you will have several options of coverage to choose from. Ask lots of questions and make sure you're clear on exactly what is being covered.

While insurance is a definite necessity, you don't want to be over-insured and hence become insurance poor. A good agent will care about your business more than he does his commissions. Search until you find that one.

Hard Money Lender

There will come a time in your business when a stupendous deal will come across your path. You've done the research and you can see this is a killer deal. But you're strapped for the needed cash to turn the deal. What to do?

This is when a hard money lender comes into the picture. When you need cash, and speed is of the essence, this is the team member you will turn to.

This lender is in the business of lending money; this is what he does – probably on a full-time basis. He will charge an arm and a leg for interest, but if it's only for a short-term then it will be worth it to you. The hard money lender doesn't care so much about your credit rating as he does about this deal – the collateral. They want to be sure that if the deal goes bad, they can recoup their money.

Here again it will be to your benefit to seek out a lender that you can work with. Find this person and establish a relationship ahead of the time that you will need these services. (It's about speed, remember.)

Having a hard money lender in your corner will give you so much more confidence as you are out there making deals. It could mean the difference between your business moving forward or growing stagnant.

(*Private money lenders* will also be in the picture when it comes to raising funds, but we'll cover that subject in a later chapter.)

Mentor

Going back to what was said at the beginning of this chapter about being entrepreneurial minded, this mindset often stops an investor from seeking help and guidance. What a loss if this is true. Having a mentor can whisk you through an immense learning curve. A good mentor can be the ultimate in the use of leverage.

This will be a person who knows the REI business, is successful in the business, and cares about the success of others. It will be someone you can easily relate to and can work well under their guidance and supervision.

Keep in mind a mentor can only take you so far and no further. If you fail to follow through with corresponding actions on a regular basis, then you are simply wasting your time and theirs.

Unlike an accountant, a lender, or an insurance agent, the mentor will not have a sign on the office door. This will be a rather obscure individual. This is why it's good to network where investors hang out. It's through these types of events that you may come in contact with a mentor.

Let it be known throughout your group that you are ready and willing to hook up with a good mentor and go from there.

When you begin working with your mentor, keep up good communication and make sure all expectations are clarified at the outset. If you get underway with a mentor and sense that it's not working out, don't be hesitant to walk away. Your time is too valuable to waste on a relationship that's not working.

In some mentor relationships, the newbie will bring a deal and get the mentor's opinion and guidance. If it's a go, the mentor may even help with funds, and then share in the profits when the property is flipped.

There are dozens of ways this relationship can work to the benefit of everyone. The most important thing is that the ground rules are clearly laid out from the get-go.

When reading through this chapter it may seem a daunting task to build your team. It's really not. The key is that you become fully aware of the importance of your team, and then to be fully intentional in your quest to find your players and make your business run like a well-oiled machine.

In the next chapter you will become versed in the need for marketing. You may or may not enjoy this subject, but that doesn't matter. It is absolutely necessary for the growth and health of your business.

Will You Be Found?

Let's say you are settled into the wholesaling niche. You are intently looking for distressed (highly-motivated) sellers so you can acquire properties and then turn around and assign the contract to a rehabber or rental-property owner. How will that distressed seller ever find you? What are you doing to market your business? Will you be found?

Realize that entire books have been written about marketing, both in general and specifically for real estate investors. We will cover the highlights in this book, but you are encouraged to do your own research in this area.

Two Basic Marketing Venues

In this age of technology, the two venues of marketing are online marketing, and off line marketing. Both have their place and both are important. It's up to you and your business model which will be your initial focus. The best thing about online is that exposure is relatively inexpensive. But then, so is putting up bandit signs. (And over the years, bandit signs repeatedly come up as a winning marketing strategy. That is, if your local laws will allow them to be posted.)

Marketing Plan

Marketing is not always the strong suit of the entrepreneur investor. Some will do a little here and a little there, but never with a planned and consistent strategy. Most are not sure where their leads are coming from, and because of that, they don't know where to intensify their actions.

Here are a few ideas to get you started:
- Create a marketing plan
- Start small
- Keep marketing expenses down (especially at the beginning)
- Be consistent
- Measure results
- Learn what's bringing in the most leads and intensify efforts in that area

Online Marketing

Website

The most important part of your online marketing will be your website. This is a must – no debate in this area. Your website will be the foundation of all other marketing that you do online.

In this day and age creating a website, or having one created for you, is simple, quick and easy.

Using WordPress (https://wordpress.com/) is the best for beginners. It offers extensive tutorials to guide the way.

Barring that, simply run a Google search for "websites for real estate investors" and see what comes up. You may be surprised that there are many options to choose from and most are easy to use an affordable.

Once you have your site up, you now have your own URL that can be used in all your social media, and in all your printed materials.

Your website can feature a *web form* whereby you can capture the visitor's contact information. Some investors will offer a free report, or a free ebook in exchange for the contact information. This information is how you build your list of contacts.

The beautiful thing about your website is that you can link it to all your social media sites. The more your URL shows up online, the greater the exposure, the higher you will rank on Google, and the easier you can be found when someone is searching for your services.

Videos

Google is the largest search engine on the Internet and YouTube is owned by Google and it's second-largest. That should speak volumes to you with regard to marketing.

Creating a video and posting it on your website is a super easy task and there's no reason for any investor to overlook this cheap marketing technique. (Did you know that videos will rank higher than websites on Google and other search engines?)

Let's say you're a rehabber. You could commandeer a friend to follow you through your newly rehabbed house. Then you upload that video on YouTube. From there, you can link it to all your social media sites. What an easy way to let the world know who you are and what you do.

Let your imagination go wild in this area. You can interview people (like your satisfied customers), you can do a self video of you explaining tips about some facet of real estate.

Look around on YouTube – do a few searches in your niche – and see what's out there. You can make this work for you, and it costs next to nothing.

Social Media

Social media includes sites such as:
- Facebook
- LinkedIn
- Twitter
- Instagram
- Pinterest

Start with Facebook and set up a *Fan Page*. This is separate and apart from your personal Facebook profile page. (Always keep personal and business separate.)

Your business Facebook fan page allows you to create posts that are scheduled for the future. This means you can set time aside once a week and create a week's worth of FB posts. You don't have to be at your computer posting FB posts each and every day. Don't reinvent the wheel.

Use FB to post clever sayings, or to post your properties that are available, or feature photos of the work you do and also feature your videos. This will be linked to your website and to other social media sites.

When you first start out, work with only one social media site. Since FB is the most popular at this time, it's best to begin there, and add another when you can fit it into your schedule. This way you will not become overwhelmed.

You might want to then set up your Twitter account and link that into Facebook. Twitter is quick and easy and doesn't demand much of your time. You'll find you can say a lot in a few words.

Move on to the other social media sites only if time permits and only if you feel the exposure is worth it.

You may want to consider outsourcing the upkeep and maintenance of your social media sites. (Hire someone to do these tasks for you.) This is a great way to leverage your time.

Ads

Many investors will tell you they could never do without their listings on Craigslist. (http://www.craigslist.org) No matter if you are looking to buy or sell houses, there's a classification and a location on Craigslist. This is an especially great site for those investors who go virtual (sell all across the country regardless of their geographic location).

The challenge with Craigslist is that your listing will quickly sink to the bottom of the list if not continually updated. This is yet another task that can be outsourced. Some investors hire a person to twice a day go in and update their Craigslist ads. This keeps the ads in view and brings in many more ad responses.

You can be assured that if you are wholesaling, the investors-buyers that you are targeting are scouring these sites everyday looking for properties in which to invest. It's like one huge market center.

You can find many other sites in which to post your ads, but Craigslist is the site of choice for most investors.

Off Line Marketing

Bandit Signs

Top of the list for marketing off of the Internet is the old standby – bandit signs. The name, as you may be aware, came about because investors would put out signs in the evening and they might be all taken down by the next morning.

Through the years bandit signs have sometimes come into disrepute, but still they prove to be powerful lead-getters! Even the big-time investors will still put out bandit signs. Why? Because they know they work.

It can be a simple sign that says something like:

We Buy Houses All Cash Close Fast
Phone #
Website URL

The response is always amazing.

Unlike posting an ad on the Internet, there will be a cost involved with these signs. However, there are many online sign companies that offer low-costs on bulk purchases.

Also involved is the time required to put out signs. This is yet another great outsource task. This could involve a high school student (one who drives and has access to a vehicle) who is looking to earn extra cash. Have them target one zip code area in which you want to focus. This could keep you busy with leads for weeks.

Postcards

When it comes to direct mail you will find there are a wide variety of approaches ranging from the well-known *yellow letter* to the hand-addressed letters. Because so few people get mail these days, direct mail marketing has once again come into its own and is proving to be very effective. However, it can be quite expensive. This is why it's best to begin with postcards.

Postcards cost less to print, require no envelope stuffing, and require less postage than a letter. The big plus is that as soon as it's taken from the mailbox, it's being read. The note can be short, letting the recipient know that you're in the market to purchase their house.

Another advantage is that the recipient many hang onto the postcard. They're not ready to sell today, but may be ready a few weeks down the line. It may be stuck on their fridge door for future reference.

When doing a mailing, you can choose a targeted list – let's say it's a list of out-of-state owners. These are often people who are looking to get rid of their property since they live too far away to keep it up properly. Such targeted mailings often have a high response rate and is well worth the cost.

Business Cards

If you think business cards have gone out of vogue, think again. The business card is like having a mini billboard.

The card should be simple in design and easy to understand. The message of what you do should be clear. On it will be your contact information which will include your website URL.

No matter where you are, or what you're doing, always be handing out business cards. This is a much overlooked marketing method and can net great results. You could give your card to someone who knows someone who needs your services. You never know. But it can't happen if the cards are still sitting in the box on your desk.

This chapter has barely scratched the surface when it comes to marketing. But there is enough here to get you focused in this direction. Your business may grow at first simply by word of mouth, but that will not last long. Marketing must be on your radar at all times.

Again, start off small; keep marketing costs down. Avoid spending the big bucks until you are making the big bucks. You can bring in a good stream of business if you perfect just a few of the strategies listed here.

Now that we've laid the foundation for a few basic investing niches, and you understand how important it is to build a team, and now that you understand the importance of marketing and getting your name out there, it's time to dig in and review more specialized niches in the investing business. We'll do that in the next chapter.

Specialized Niches

Some investors begin as a bird dog. It is the exact niche that fits them; they get good at it and stay there. It meets their needs and they enjoy offering such a great service to investors.

Other investors love wholesaling and stay in that niche. The same for rehabbers – the world of fix-and-flip fits them perfectly.

[*As a side note, I hope you're getting the gist of why it's important to know who you are, and exactly what you want. Otherwise you'll be following the lead of some guru and you'll be miserable because what they are doing doesn't fit you, or your needs, or your goals.*]

Still other investors are enamored with some of the more complex investing niches. We're going to review a few of those in this chapter.

We've now moved past the discussion of if you're looking for fast cash or long-term wealth. We're now into looking into specialized areas of real estate investing.

Pre-Foreclosures

A property is considered to be in pre-foreclosure once the defaulted loan is recorded in the public records. This then opens a short window of time which could range from 90 days to 10 months in which you can step into the picture. Each state is different and it depends on their laws and proceedings. Eventually it winds up at a public auction. (Sometimes called a trustee sale.)

This can spell panic time for the homeowner. If the foreclosure goes through they have not only lost the home but it will have a negative effect on their credit.

As you can imagine, ever since the RE bust in 2007, investors have rushed into this niche. Some have perfected this area and have learned exactly how to work with sellers to protect their dignity and still make a concerted effort to create a win-win outcome for everyone concerned.

Foreclosures (REOs)

Moving from pre-foreclosure to actual foreclosed properties requires more skill and knowledge. This is because you must deal with the lender. These negotiations can take a long time because it travels through several layers of approval processes.

The bank will offer little or no information about the condition of the property. This means the investor must pay for a professional home inspection of the property in order to know the state of the property.

Earnest money will also be required to show the buyer's interest in the property. If there are title issues, they must be addressed and resolved.

Foreclosed properties can be purchased at auction; but they can also be purchased through an agent to specialize in these properties.

Once the intricacies of this niche are learned it can be extremely lucrative.

Short Sales

In the case of someone losing their home, there will be situations where the person owes more on the house than it's worth. This is due to the often-reckless loans that were issued where the borrower got a loan that covered closing costs in addition to the price of the house. Soon they are in over their heads and can't sell.

Sometimes the lender is willing to accept less than what is due – and this is known as a *short sale*.

Those who learn this niche can make a massive income. It requires a steep learning curve since it involves a lot of negotiating and a lot of paperwork.

The investor in the short sale niche will be dealing with what's known as the *Loss Mitigation Department* in the lending institution. This requires lengthy phone calls, making your way through the phone mazes, and being placed on hold for long periods of time. It's not for the faint of heart.

Basically, the lender knows that a short sale will save them hundreds of dollars in costs. The investor who is skilled in this area is able to convince the lender that it's not worth it for them to continue to hold the property.

The investor must supply extensive information regarding the property (its condition and repair costs), and information about the owner's financial situation.

The person in this niche loves nitty-gritty details – they see the entire scenario as one huge puzzle that needs solving. Investors who become knowledgeable in this niche can often move up into the luxury-home market and make huge sums of money on one short sale alone.

Tax Liens

Have you ever heard stories of investors who have been able to pick up properties for pennies on the dollar because they bought the tax lien? It's not a far-fetched tale. It can, and does happen. This is yet another specialized niche in real estate investing.

This niche is a bit tricky so it's advisable to enter in here with a knowledgeable mentor who can guide the way.

These properties become available because the owner fails to pay the taxes on the property. The county files a lawsuit against them and if the taxes aren't paid, a public auction is held and the property goes to the highest bidder.

Let's say you win the bid and purchase the tax certificate. You now acquire the rights that are held by the county. Following this purchase the owner still has a period of time in which he can redeem his property. This is a varied amount of time ranging from a few months to a few years.

If this redemption of the property never happens, you are now the owner of the property, no matter how much (or how little) you bid. Some have bid as little as $1,300 and purchased a house worth $130,000.

Pretty amazing way to buy properties and build a RE investing business.

There are yet other specialized niches in the world of real estate investing, but this gives you a good idea of what's available and where this journey could take you.

At some point you may feel you're ready to move on to bigger things. In the next chapter you'll get a look at owning multi-family properties.

Scaling Up

If your niche is in the buy-and-hold, long-term wealth building strategy, you may soon begin to look for something larger than a single-family dwelling. It may be time to consider multi-family properties. You'll be looking at a greater investment, and yet a greater opportunity for cash flow.

This is not to be confused with sprawling apartment complexes. This is referring to structures that may have 2, 4, 6, and perhaps 8 families under the same roof. At first this may seem a little intimidating. This is why it comes later in the book. Hopefully you will have been laying a strong foundation in your business before you reach this point. That being said, let's look at a few reasons why this might be a wise investing decision.

Loan Qualification

Let's say you're looking at a four-plex to purchase. First of all, the lender will look at the potential income on the property as part of the qualification purposes. That will never happen when you purchase a single-family property.

Economy of Scale

Another point to be considered in a multi-unit building is called *economy of scale.* If you purchase four rental properties, you have four separate houses that require upkeep. There will be four roofs and four lawns to care for; there will be four tenants spread out in different areas – perhaps different neighborhoods.

On the other hand, if you purchase a four-plex you have one roof and one lawn to care for, and all your tenants are in one central location. Now the economy of scale is working in your favor.

Cash Flow

The one aspect that will make you the happiest is the increased cash flow. Your overhead will be less so your profits will be greater. If you purchase several multi-family units soon your income will allow you to take on a property manager. This will then lessen your work load and add to your quality of life.

Reduced Risk

As the owner of several separate rental properties, if one tenant leaves you are faced with a loss of income for that house. You are then faced with cleanup to prepare for a new tenant, advertising to find a new tenant, while still paying the mortgage and the utilities.

If you own a multi-family property, one tenant may leave, but the ongoing expense is much less – plus you have the income from all the other units coming in.

A Road Less Traveled

You will find your competition among other investors is much less in this niche. They might see the big price tag, and think of all the work involved, and as a result will shy away. This is to your advantage.

As you move into this realm you'll soon find that the negotiations and buy-and-sell process is not that much different, but the end results are totally different.

How to Begin

One of the best ways to begin in this niche is to study the market in your area. Find what types of neighborhoods are best for multi-family properties. Check out the typical rent for the area.

Start small. You may want to think about starting with a duplex. Some investors have been known to purchase a duplex and live in one side while renting out the other. This is a great way to get income started and keep living expenses down. It's as simple to get financing for a duplex as it is a single-dwelling home.

As you move in this direction, this is a great niche in which to have a knowledgeable mentor by your side. Find a mentor who deals in multi-family properties and allow the mentor to walk you through the steps. You'll be much less likely to make any major mistakes.

Wide-Open Field

You may know a lot of investors who are flipping houses, rehabbing houses, and even buying and holding houses, but how many do you know who are consistently building up an inventory of multi-family properties? Probably not many.

If this sounds like an area that might appeal to you get buy and do your homework. The door of opportunity is wide open and the field is sparse. There's definitely room for you.

Money and funding have been mentioned sporadically throughout the book. Now it's time to dig in and learn more about how your deals might be funded. This fascinating subject is covered in the next chapter.

Show Me the Money

When the subjects of bird dogging and wholesaling were discussed in the first of the book, the key point was that either one can be done with very little cash investment. And, as was mentioned, this is a good way to build up cash reserves.

However, most investors soon want to graduate up from those niches. They are now well able to sniff out deals and the time will come when a deal is just so good that flipping it is no longer the desired end result. This investor wants to invest in this property. But how? Where does the money come from?

Hard Money Lender

In the chapter on building your team, we discussed the need for a hard money lender. You may want to go back and revisit that section. You learned that while a hard money lender may charge a high rate of interest, still if the deal is a highly lucrative one, it will be well worth that extra interest you will have to pay. You can consider it the "cost of doing business."

You will want to seek out this person long before the need arises, and then build a good working relationship. When you know you have this team member as your backup, you will have a greater degree of confidence as you are out there making offers to motivated sellers.

A word of caution: use the hard money lender only for rare circumstances. The deal must be worth the extra cost involved. Also go this route only when you have a substantial buyer's list built up. This way, you know you can find a buyer for the deal and can flip it quickly. That way the loan will be paid off quickly. You want to build up a good reputation with this lender. That reputation will stand you in good stead in future days.

Private Money Lender

A private money lender is probably one of the most creative ways to fund your deals, and finding these lenders is relatively simple. Unlike a hard money lender, these are people who may know little about the subject of finance, and even less about real estate investing.

What they do have is what's known as *lazy money*. They have money that is invested, but is bringing in a small return – and they're usually quite dissatisfied with the returns they are getting.

You come on the scene and lay out a plan whereby they fund your deal and will then earn a much greater return on investment than what they are currently receiving. This could be your mother-in-law, or your co-worker, or someone you met at your local REIA meeting. (The latter would know a bit more about real estate investing...) It could be most anyone.

When you first approach the candidate you may not have a deal in hand; however, you have closed a few deals in the past. You can show them exactly how it works and give them an idea how long it might take for them to receive the return on their investment. Working with private lenders means you can move quickly since you will not have piles of forms to submit as you do with other lending situations.

Make your terms clear at the outset. Explain exactly what you're offering. People seem to be the most receptive to a return of about 8% to 12%; anything higher and they tend to think it must be a scam. (The too-good-to-be-true thinking.)

When a deal does come your way, and you need the investor to come into the picture, present the deal as specifically as you can. Leave nothing out. This person must be well informed. No surprises.

When lining out the time frame for the loan, always set it up for longer than you think you will need. It's so much better to have time left over than to run out of time. You will be more comfortable if you have a built-in safety net.

Payment

When you first get to know this lender one of the questions you will ask is when they would like to be paid? It could be monthly, or quarterly, or even annually. Your goal is to get to know your lender and meet that person's needs and expectations as best you can. Find out what they are looking for and what will meet their needs.

Let's say your private money lender has agreed (for a specific deal) to loan you $100,000 note for 12 months at 8% per annum. You specify that there will be no prepayment penalty, that way if you close the deal sooner than expected you can make the payoff with no extra fees. You will then add the option of a possible extension for 3 month. (This is your safety net.) Last but not least, you stipulate that you will make monthly interest payments.

You will simply divide the 8% of 100,000 by 12 to come up with the monthly interest payments. This can be a bookkeeping headache, but for a first-time lender it's a great way to make a good impression. They get to see quick results.

Once you build a good relationship built on trust, you may be able to revert to an annual payment. Same as before – the loan is $100,000 at 8% per annum. At the end of the 12 months, you make the payout to that lender plus the 8% interest in one lump sum.

The Many Benefits

There are so many benefits to having private money lenders you can hardly list them all. You can do more deals; you can earn more cash flow; you have more confidence knowing the cash is there; the lender is pleased and once the payback is made they want to immediately invest again; and then – word begins to spread. Instead of looking for private money investors, they will have heard the stories and they will come to you.

Partnership (Joint Venture)

A joint venture partnership entails joining forces with another investor. This may be one who is more experienced and more knowledgeable about the world of RE investing than you are.

This individual has more cash reserves than you do, but you have more time. You will be the one who does the footwork, and possibly even the rehabbing. The partner will be the one who approves (or in some cases does not approve) the deals that are brought to him.

Once the deal closes the profits are split equally. This is a great way to learn the business, to walk though a buy-and-sell experience with a shared risk. At the same time you are gaining credibility, something you will need for future deals. It will also serve you well when you're ready to go to hard money lenders (or even private lenders) on your own.

The bottom line is the bottom line! You have an avenue that allows you to earn cash and then leverage up in your business.

Splitting the proceeds may seem pretty steep at first. But, after all, half of something is better than all of nothing. Consider it the price of doing business – take it to the bank and move on.

If you are serious about getting into the field of real estate investing, you need never let a lack of money, or funding, be the obstacle that stops you! In this chapter you have seen three options for getting funding, but there are so many more. Get creative and think outside the box. When you do, that's when your business will grow by leaps and bound!

Conclusion

I trust that this has been not only an educational journey for you, but also an enjoyable one.

You now know and understand that it's not necessary to have money, or to go into debt, to get started in this business. You now know that you can start small simply by bird dogging and earning extra cash while learning the basics of wholesaling.

You also have seen that there's no such thing as one way (or one secret key ingredient), to success in real estate investing. The only right way to achieve success is the way that is right for you. And you will never know which way is right for you until you know exactly where you are now, where you want to go, and how you will get there.

The more you are in the business, the more you will know the niche that most appeals to you – the one that will be the best fit for you. (Not what some so-called guru says is the best way.)

You are more aware now whether you want to stay in the quick-cash-flow arena, or move up into the long-range, wealth-building arena. You are equipped to make an informed decision according to what's best for you and your goals.

Along the way you've learned more about how important marketing is to your business and how to start with a small budget and work your way up.

How and when to build your team was also presented to you. This is something you can take action with immediately. No need to wait.

Several specialized niches were introduced to you, any one of which might be right up your alley. Now you're aware that more options are out there, you have more choices.

Expanding from single-family properties over into multi-family properties may appeal to you. Now you know the advantages of taking that step.

Additionally, you are now aware that there are a variety of ways in which to procure funds to snag those prime deals. It doesn't have to be your money. And in the case of a joint venture, it doesn't even have to be all your own risk.

The world of real estate investing is an exciting one and full of potential and great possibilities. It can be a world where you find great adventure and great rewards. But if approached in the wrong way, with the wrong mindset, and the wrong goals, it can spell disaster.

You are now armed with truth and facts – you destiny will be the former and not the latter.

Good luck to you in all your ventures!

Made in the USA
Middletown, DE
23 February 2016